LOSE

THE
SLOW COOKER
SPICE
GUY/CURRY
DIET
RECIPE BOOK

Fragrant Low-Calorie Easy & Healthy
Curries
From Around The World
For Beginners

**Lose Weight Fast
The Slow Cooker Spice G̲ ̲ ̲ ̲ Diet Recipe Book
Fragrant Low-Calorie Easy He̲ ̲thy Curries From Around
The World For Beginners**

Copyright © Iota Publishing 2018
All rights reserved. This book or any portion thereof may not be reproduced or used in any manner whatsoever without the express written permission of the publisher.

ISBN: 9781913005221

Disclaimer

The content of this book is also available under the title 'The Skinny Slow Cooker Curry Recipe Book' by CookNation. Except for use in any review, the reproduction or utilisation of this work in whole or in part in any form by any electronic, mechanical or other means, now known or hereafter invented, including xerography, photocopying and recording, or in any information storage or retrieval system, is forbidden without the permission of the publisher.

This book is sold subject to the condition that it shall not, by way of trade or otherwise, be lent, resold, hired out or otherwise circulated without the prior consent of the publisher in any form of binding or cover other than that in which it is published and without a similar condition including this condition being imposed on the subsequent purchaser.

This book is designed to provide information on meals that can be made in line with the principals of the Blood Sugar Diet. Some recipes may contain nuts or traces of nuts. Those suffering from any allergies associated with nuts should avoid any recipes containing nuts or nut based oils.

This information is provided and sold with the knowledge that the publisher and author do not offer any legal or other professional advice.
In the case of a need for any such expertise consult with the appropriate professional.
This book does not contain all information available on the subject, and other sources of recipes are available.

Every effort has been made to make this book as accurate as possible. However, there may be typographical and or content errors. Therefore, this book should serve only as a general guide and not as the ultimate source of subject information.
This book contains information that might be dated and is intended only to educate and entertain.

The author and publisher shall have no liability or responsibility to any person or entity regarding any loss or damage incurred, or alleged to have incurred, directly or indirectly, by the information contained in this book.

Contents

Introduction	**7**
Preparation	10
Low Cost	10
Slow Cooker Tips	11
Our Recipes	12
I'm Already On A Diet. Can I Use These Recipes?	12
I Am Only Cooking For One. Will This Book Work For Me?	13
Nutrition	13
Portion Sizes	14
Side Dishes	14
Meat Curries	**17**
Thai Basil Curry	18
Thyme Steak Curry	19
Moroccan Lamb & Apricot Curry	20
Hot Spiced Creamy Beef Curry	21
Pork & Cardamom Curry	22
Thai Beef Curry	23
Spiced Seed Pork Curry	24
Caribbean Beef Curry	25
Beef & Almond Curry	26
Pea & Beef Curry	27
Korean Beef & Potato Curry	28
Lemongrass & Pork Coconut Curry	29
Beef & Red Pepper Kofta Curry	30
Marrakesh Lime & Lamb Curry	31
St. Bart's Pork Curry	32
Spiced Meatball Curry	33
Hot Bamboo Shoot Beef Curry	34
Lamb Jalfrezi	35
Beef Madras	36
Poultry Curries	**37**
Fiery Chicken Curry	38
Chicken & Almond Curry	39

Contents

Chicken & Soy Curry	40
Rogan Josh	41
Chicken & Butternut Squash Curry	42
Sweet Potato & Chicken Curry	43
Chicken Keema	44
Garam Masala Chicken Curry	45
Chicken & Tamarind Curry	46
Chicken & Mango Curry	47
Thai Chicken Pieces	48
Fresh Tomato & Basil Chicken Curry	49
'Butter' Chicken	50
Chicken Bhuna	51
Chicken Dopiaza	52
Garlic Chicken	53
Chicken Korma	54
Tandoori Chicken	55
Simple Creamy Chicken Curry	56
Dhansak	57
Chicken Pasanda	58
Chicken & Split Pea Curry	59
Seafood Curries	**61**
King Prawn Masala	62
King Prawn & Fresh Pea Curry	63
Paka Hua Alu	64
Thai Fish Curry	65
Ginger & Fresh Tomato Prawns	66
Mackerel Curry	67
Coconut Milk & Fish Curry	68
Pineapple & Prawn Curry	69
Fresh Mussel Curry	70
Vegetable Curries	**71**
Aloo Gobi	72
Simple Vegetable Curry	73
Saag Aloo	74
Masaruma & Tomato Curry	75

Contents

Broccoli & Mini Corn Curry	76
Thai Squash & Coconut Curry	77
Coriander & Sweet Potato Curry	78
Spinach & Paneer	79
Cumin & Spinach Potatoes	80
Egg Curry	81
Chickpea Curry	82
Red Lentil & Courgette Curry	83
Munga Curry	84
Onion & Egg Masala	85
Aloo Cauliflower Curry	86
Plantain & Sweet Onion Curry	87
Garlic Curry	88
Gobhi Coconut Curry	89
Green Beans & Fenugreek Curry	90
Cauliflower 'Rice'	91
Conversion Chart	**92**
Other Titles	**95**

The Slow Cooker Spice Guy Curry Diet
Recipe Book

INTRODUCTION

Introduction

Welcome to *Lose Weight Fast: The Slow Cooker Spice Guy Curry Diet Recipe Book.*

Curry has become one of the most loved dishes around the world. Subtle blends of spices that create mouth watering meals reminiscent of the East. Whether you love meat, fish or prefer vegetarian options, there is a curry to suit you. Hot, mild, fragrant, sweet or nutty, the choices are endless. Every country, city and home has their own version of how to make a curry. That's the wonderful thing about cooking with spices, you can experiment to suit your own taste buds and provided you adhere to a few basic principals, you can't really go wrong. While many restaurant style curries are served within minutes of ordering, the slow cooker method allows the full flavour of all the ingredients to penetrate every part of the dish giving maximum flavour to your meal and filling your home with the incredible aroma of a Delhi spice market.

Our recipes are inspired from around the world including more traditional dishes like Korma, Thai Green Curry, Saag Aloo & Rogan Josh, but also a multitude of inspirational easy to prepare curries that will satisfy every palate.

It is easy to be overwhelmed by the idea of cooking curries. With the cuisine relying so heavily on spice blends you can be put off by the vast array on offer before you've even started. Don't be afraid of spices - you'll get to know them quickly and become confident in your cooking in no time. The *Slow Cooker Spice Guy Curry Diet Recipe Book* introduces a handful of key spices which you can use time and time again throughout the book and which, once bought, you can keep in the store cupboard and go back to month after month saving you money in the long run.

The slow cooker allows you to prepare delicious curries with the minimum of preparation and fuss. With as little as just 15 minutes preparation you can have a low calorie, nutritious and tasty curry slowly cooking whilst you get on with the things you need to do. If you have a family to cook for, a busy life that means you start early and are out for most of the day, or just don't want to be tied to the kitchen for hours, then the slow cooker is your saviour. Slow cooking enables you to effortlessly prepare meals without worrying that your food will overcook, spill-over or burn. The slow cooking process brings out the best of the ingredients without losing out on goodness. It's easy to use, delivers great results and, with our skinny slow cooker curry recipes, you can be confident you are preparing low calorie & healthy dishes as part of a wholesome diet.

If you have already read one of our other low calorie titles, you may be familiar with some of the following information, in which case please feel free to skip straight to our recipes. If however your slow cooker has been stored in a cupboard for months or you have just purchased a slow cooker for the first time, we recommend reading the following pages to familiarise yourself with how to get the best out of your appliance and advice on using our recipes.

During the colder months our bodies naturally crave warm, filling and comforting food, which can often result in overeating, weight gain and sluggishness.

These delicious curry recipes use simple and inexpensive fresh and store-cupboard ingredients, are packed full of flavour & goodness, and show that you can enjoy maximum taste with minimum calories. All our curry recipes use ingredients that are readily available in most supermarkets so there is no need to source from specialist outlets.

Each recipe has been tried, tested, and enjoyed time and time again. We hope you will find these dishes both delicious and inspirational and perfect to keep count of your calories.

Preparation
All the recipes should take no longer than 10-15 minutes to prepare. Browning the meat will make a difference to the taste of your recipe, but if you really don't have the time, don't worry - it will still taste great.

All meat and vegetables should be cut into even sized pieces unless stated in the recipes. Some ingredients can take longer to cook than others, particularly root vegetables, but that has been allowed for in the cooking time.

As much as possible, meat should be trimmed of visible fat and the skin removed.

Low Cost
Slow cooking is ideal for cheaper meat cuts. The 'tougher' cuts used in this collection of recipes are transformed into meat which melts-in-your-mouth and helps to keep costs down. We've also made sure not to include too many one-off ingredients, which are used for a single recipe and never

used again. All the herbs and spices listed can be used in multiple recipes throughout the book.

Slow Cooker Tips

- All cooking times are a guide. Make sure you get to know your own slow cooker so that you can adjust timings accordingly.
- Read the manufacturers operating instructions as appliances can vary. For example, some recommend preheating the slow cooker for 20 minutes before use whilst others advocate switching on only when you are ready to start cooking.
- Slow cookers do not brown meat. While this is not always necessary, if you do prefer to brown your meat you must first do this in a pan with a little low calorie cooking spray.
- A spray of low calorie cooking oil in the cooker before adding ingredients will help with cleaning or you can buy liners.
- Don't be tempted to regularly lift the lid of your appliance while cooking. The seal that is made with the lid on is all part of the slow cooking process. Each time you do lift the lid you may need to increase the cooking time.
- Removing the lid at the end of the cooking time can be useful to thicken up a sauce by adding additional cooking time and continuing to cook without the lid on. On the other hand if the sauce it too thick removing the lid and adding a little more liquid can help.
- Where possible always add hot liquids to your slow cooker, not cold.
- Do not overfill your slow cooker.
- Allow the inner dish of your slow cooker to completely cool before cleaning. Any stubborn marks can usually be removed after a period of soaking in hot soapy water.

- Be confident with your cooking. Feel free to use substitutes to suit your own taste and don't let a missing herb or spice stop you making a meal - you'll almost always be able to find something to replace it.

Our Recipes
The recipes in this book are all low calorie curry dishes serving 4, which makes it easier for you to monitor your overall daily calorie intake as well as those you are cooking for.
The recommended daily calories are approximately 2000 for women and 2500 for men.

Broadly speaking, by consuming the recommended levels of calories each day you should maintain your current weight. Reducing the number of calories (a calorie deficit) will result in losing weight. This happens because the body begins to use fat stores for energy to make up the reduction in calories, which in turn results in weight loss. We have already counted the calories for each dish making it easy for you to fit this into your daily eating plan whether you want to lose weight, maintain your current figure or are just looking for some great-tasting, skinny slow cooker curries.

I'm Already On A Diet. Can I Use These Recipes?
Yes of course. All the curry recipes can be great accompaniments to many of the popular calorie-counting diets. We all know that sometimes dieting can result in hunger pangs, cravings and boredom from eating the same old foods day in and day out. Our skinny slow cooker curry recipes provide filling meals that should satisfy you for hours afterwards.

I Am Only Cooking For One. Will This Book Work For Me?
Yes. We would recommend following the method for 4 servings then dividing and storing the rest in single size portions for you to use in the future. Most of the recipes will freeze well. Allow all food to cool to room temperature before refrigerating or freezing. When ready to defrost, allow to thaw in a fridge overnight then at room temperature for a few hours depending on the size of the portion. Reheat thoroughly.

Nutrition
All of the recipes in this collection are balanced low calorie meals that should keep you feeling full and help you avoid snacking in-between meals.

If you are following a diet, it is important to balance your food between proteins, good carbs, dairy, fruit and vegetables.

- **Protein.** Keeps you feeling full and is also essential for building body tissue. Good protein sources come from meat, fish and eggs.
- **Carbohydrates.** Carbs are generally high in calories, which makes them difficult to include in a calorie limiting diet. However carbs are a good source of energy for your body as they are converted more easily into glucose (sugar), providing energy. Try to eat 'good carbs' which are high in fibre and nutrients e.g. whole fruits and veg, nuts, seeds, wholegrain cereals, beans and legumes.
- **Dairy.** Dairy products provide you with vitamins and minerals. Cheeses can be high in calories but other products such as fat free Greek yoghurt, crème fraiche and skimmed milk are all good.

- **Fruit & Vegetables.** Eat your five a day. There is never a better time to fill your 5 a day quota. Not only are fruit and veg healthy, they also fill up your plate and are ideal snacks when you are feeling hungry.

We have adopted the broader nutritional principals in all our recipes.

Portion Sizes
The majority of recipes are for 4 servings. The calorie count is based on one serving. It is important to remember that if you are aiming to lose weight using any of our skinny curry recipes, the size of the portion that you put on your plate will significantly affect your weight loss efforts. Filling your plate with over-sized portions will obviously increase your calorie intake and hamper your dieting efforts.

It is important with all meals that you use a correct sized portion, which is generally the size of your clenched fist. This applies to any side dishes of vegetables and carbs too.

Side Dishes
All the curries in this book fall under 200, 300 & 400 calories. You may choose to serve with a side dish depending on your diet. Traditionally side dishes of bread and rice can be loaded with calories so we have offered a couple of different options.

Each side serves 4. The calories noted are PER SERVING. Here is a guide to those sides:

- 200g/7oz basmati rice   *140 calories*
- 200g/7oz fine egg noodles   *120 calories*

- 200g/7oz cauliflower rice   *50 calories (recipe p.91)*
- 300g/11oz plain green salad   *15 calories*

All Recipes Are A Guide Only
All the recipes in this book are a guide only. You may need to alter quantities and cooking times to suit your own appliances.

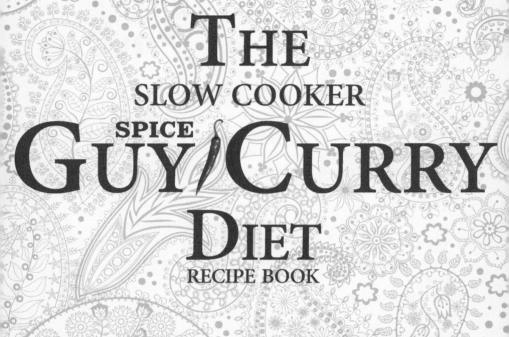

THE SLOW COOKER SPICE GUY CURRY DIET
RECIPE BOOK

MEAT CURRIES

Thai Basil Curry
Serves 4

Ingredients:

500g/1lb 2oz pork tenderloin, cubed
2 onions, finely chopped
2 tbsp Thai red curry paste
2 tsp tamarind paste
½ tsp ground coriander/cilantro
1 red pepper, sliced
2 carrots, sliced into batons
1 lemongrass stalk, finely chopped
3 tbsp freshly chopped basil
500ml/2 cups chicken stock/broth
Salt & pepper to taste
Low cal cooking oil spray

Method:

- Season the pork and quickly brown for a couple of minutes in a frying pan with a little low cal oil.
- Remove from the heat and place in the slow cooker along with all the other ingredients.
- Combine well, cover and leave to cook on low for 5-7 hours or until the pork is tender and cooked through.

- For side dish options see page 14

Tamarind paste is made from the tart fruit of the Tamarind tree. It is regularly used in curry as a spicy souring agent.

Thyme Steak Curry

Serves 4

Method:

- First mix the curry powder and tomato puree together to form a paste.
- Season the steak and quickly brown for a couple of minutes in a frying pan with a little low cal oil.
- Remove from the heat and place in the slow cooker along with all the other ingredients.

Combine well, cover and leave to cook on low for 5-7 hours or until the steak is tender and cooked through.

- For side day options see page 14

Ingredients:

500g/1lb 2oz lean sirloin steak, thickly sliced
1 tbsp medium curry powder
3 tbsp tomato puree/paste
2 onions, finely chopped
2 garlic cloves, crushed
1 tbsp dried thyme
2 carrots, sliced into batons
150g/5oz sweet potato, diced
2 celery stalks, chopped
500ml/2 cups beef stock/broth
Salt & pepper to taste
Low cal cooking oil spray

You could cook this dish on high for 3-4 hours f you prefer. Reduce the stock by 25% if you do so.

Moroccan Lamb & Apricot Curry
Serves 4

Ingredients:

500g/1lb 2oz lean lamb fillet, cubed
2 onions, finely chopped
2 garlic cloves, crushed
400g/14oz fresh chopped tomatoes
100g/3½oz dried apricots, finely chopped
½ tsp each ground ginger, turmeric, coriander/cilantro & paprika
A pinch each of ground cinnamon, nutmeg & salt
2 carrots, sliced into batons
120ml/ ½ cup vegetable stock/broth
Salt & pepper to taste
Low cal cooking oil spray

Method:

- Season the lamb and quickly brown for a couple of minutes in a frying pan with a little low cal oil.
- Remove from the heat and place in the slow cooker along with all the other ingredients.
- Combine well, cover and leave to cook on low for 5-7 hours or until the lamb is tender and cooked through.

- For side dish options see page 14

Make sure the lamb is trimmed of as much visible fat as possible.

Hot Spiced Creamy Beef Curry
Serves 4

330 CALORIES PER SERVING

Method:

- Season the beef and quickly brown for a couple of minutes in a frying pan with a little low cal oil.
- Remove from the heat and place in the slow cooker along with all the other ingredients except the Greek yoghurt.
- Combine well, cover and leave to cook on low for 5-8 hours or until the beef is tender and cooked through.
- Add the yoghurt to the slow cooker. Gently stir through and serve.

- For side dish options see page 14

Add a little more beef stock or water during cooking if needed.

Ingredients:

500g/1lb 2oz lean stewing steak, cubed
1 onion, finely chopped
2 garlic cloves, crushed
1 tbsp hot curry powder
2 tbsp tomato puree/paste
2 tsp freshly grated root ginger
½ tsp ground cinnamon (optional)
2 celery stalks, chopped
250ml/1 cup beef stock/broth
120ml/½ cup fat free Greek yoghurt
Salt & pepper to taste
Low cal cooking oil spray

Pork & Cardamom Curry
Serves 4

300 CALORIES PER SERVING

Ingredients:

500g/1lb 2oz pork tenderloin, cubed
2 onions, finely chopped
1 red pepper, sliced
2 carrots, sliced into batons
3 garlic cloves, crushed
5 black cardamom pods, crushed
1 tbsp mild curry powder
2 tsp each tamarind paste & cider vinegar
250ml/1 cup chicken stock/broth
120ml/½ cup low fat coconut milk
2 spring onions/scallions, cut into thin ribbons
Salt & pepper to taste
Low cal cooking oil spray

Method:

- Season the pork and quickly brown for a couple of minutes in a frying pan with a little low cal oil.
- Remove from the heat and place in the slow cooker along with all the other ingredients except the coconut milk & spring onions.
- Combine well, cover and leave to cook on low for 4-6 hours or until the pork is tender and cooked through.
- Add the coconut milk to the slow cooker. Gently stir through and serve with the spring onions as a garnish.

- For side dish options see page 14

Cardamon is a highly prized spice. Only saffron and vanilla are more expensive per gram.

Thai Beef Curry
Serves 4

Method:

- Season the steak and quickly brown for a couple of minutes in a frying pan with a little low cal oil.
- Remove from the heat and place in the slow cooker along with all the other ingredients except the coconut cream.
- Combine well, cover and leave to cook on high for 3-5 hours or until the steak is tender and cooked through. Add the coconut cream to the slow cooker. Gently stir through and serve.

- For side dish options see page 14

You could substitute sugar snap peas or mange tout for green beans in this dish if you prefer.

Ingredients:

500g/1lb 2oz lean sirloin steak, thickly sliced
2 tbsp Thai green curry paste
1 red onion, sliced
2 garlic cloves, crushed
1 red pepper, sliced
2 tsp dried basil
1 tbsp each Thai fish sauce, lime juice & soy sauce
250ml/1 cup beef stock/broth
150g/5oz trimmed green beans
1 tbsp coconut cream
Salt & pepper to taste
Low cal cooking oil spray

Spiced Seed Pork Curry
Serves 4

Ingredients:

500g/1lb 2oz pork tenderloin, cubed
2 tsp sunflower oil
2 onions, finely chopped
2 garlic cloves, crushed
1 tbsp each cumin & coriander/cilantro seeds
1 red pepper, sliced
1 tbsp medium curry powder
1 tbsp white wine vinegar
1 tsp salt
250ml/1 cup chicken stock/broth
120ml/½ cup low fat coconut milk
2 spring onions/scallions, cut into thin ribbons
Salt & pepper to taste
Low cal cooking oil spray

Method:

- Season the pork and quickly brown for a couple of minutes in a frying pan with a little low cal oil.
- Remove from the heat and place in the slow cooker. Add the sunflower oil, onions, garlic, cumin & coriander seeds to the same frying pan and gently sauté for a few minutes until the seeds begin to pop.
- Add the contents of the pan to the slow cooker along with all the other ingredients except the coconut milk & spring onions.
- Combine well, cover and leave to cook on low for 4-6 hours or until the pork is tender and cooked through. Add the coconut milk to the slow cooker. Gently stir through and serve with the spring onions as a garnish.

- For side dish options see page 14

The cumin and coriander seeds will create a lovely aroma when sautéed to form a fragrant base to the dish.

Caribbean Beef Curry

Serves 4

Method:

- Season the steak and quickly brown for a couple of minutes in a frying pan with a little low cal oil.
- Remove from the heat and place in the slow cooker along with all the other ingredients except the coconut cream.
- Combine well, cover and leave to cook on low for 6-8 hours or until the beef is tender and cooked through. Add the coconut cream to the slow cooker. Gently stir through and serve.

- For side dish options see page 14

This curry is also nice with a little mixed spice added to give a fragrant finish to the dish.

Ingredients:

500g/1lb 2oz lean beef stewing steak, cubed
1 tbsp hot curry powder
1 red chilli, finely chopped
1 tbsp tomato puree/paste
400g/14oz tinned chopped tomatoes
2 onions, sliced
3 garlic cloves, crushed
1 tbsp dried thyme
150g/5oz sweet potato, diced
60ml/¼ cup beef stock/broth
1 tbsp coconut cream
Salt & pepper to taste
Low cal cooking oil spray

Beef & Almond Curry
Serves 4

Ingredients:

500g/1lb 2oz lean beef stewing steak, cubed
½ tsp each ground turmeric, coriander/cilantro, paprika, ginger, mild curry powder, garam masala & salt
1 red chilli, finely chopped
1 tbsp tomato puree/paste
120ml/ ½ cup tomato passata/sieved tomatoes
1 tbsp ground almonds
2 onions, sliced
3 garlic cloves, crushed
120ml/ ½ cup beef stock/broth
2 tbsp fat free Greek yoghurt
Salt & pepper to taste
Low cal cooking oil spray

Method:

- Season the beef and quickly brown for a couple of minutes in a frying pan with a little low cal oil.
- Remove from the heat and place in the slow cooker along with all the other ingredients except the yoghurt.
- Combine well, cover and leave to cook on low for 6-8 hours or until the beef is tender and cooked through. Add the yoghurt to the slow cooker. Gently stir through and serve.

- For side dish options see page 14

You could use chopped tomatoes rather than passata for this dish if you like.

Pea & Beef Curry

Serves 4

Method:

- Season the mince and quickly brown for a couple of minutes in a frying pan with a little low cal oil.
- Remove from the heat and place in the slow cooker along with all the other ingredients.
Combine well, cover and leave to cook on high for 3-5 hours or until the mince is tender and cooked through.

- For side dish options see page 14

This should be a fairly dry dish so leave to cook for longer if necessary.

Ingredients:

500g/1lb 2oz lean beef mince
2 onions, sliced
3 garlic cloves, crushed
½ tsp each ground turmeric, cumin, coriander/cilantro, paprika, ginger, medium curry powder, garam masala & salt
1 red chilli, finely chopped
200g/7oz frozen peas
120ml/½ cup tomato passata/sieved tomatoes
60ml/¼ cup beef stock/broth
2 tbsp tomato puree/paste
Salt & pepper to taste
Low cal cooking oil spray

Korean Beef & Potato Curry
Serves 4

Ingredients:

500g/1lb 2oz lean beef stewing steak
2 onions, sliced
2 garlic cloves, crushed
1 tsp turmeric
½ tsp each ground cumin, coriander/cilantro, hot chilli powder & paprika
A pinch of ground ginger, salt & garam masala
200g/7oz new potatoes, thickly sliced
200g/7oz spinach leaves
200g/7oz vine ripened tomatoes, roughly chopped
120ml/½ cup beef stock/broth
1 tbsp tomato puree/paste
Salt & pepper to taste
Low cal cooking oil spray

Method:

- Season the beef and quickly brown for a couple of minutes in a frying pan with a little low cal oil.
- Remove from the heat and place in the slow cooker along with all the other ingredients.
- Combine well, cover and leave to cook on low for 6-8 hours or until the beef is tender and cooked through.

- For side dish options see page 14

Tinned chopped tomatoes are also fine for this recipe if you don't have fresh tomatoes to hand.

Lemongrass & Pork Coconut Curry
Serves 4

Method:

- Season the pork and place in the slow cooker along with all the other ingredients except the coconut milk.
- Combine well, cover and leave to cook on high for 3-5 hours or until the pork is tender and cooked through.
- Remove the curry leaves and add the coconut milk to the slow cooker. Gently stir through and serve.

- For side dish options see page 14

A little freshly chopped coriander makes a nice garnish for this dish.

Ingredients:

500g/1lb 2oz pork tenderloin, diced
2 onions, sliced
2 garlic cloves, crushed
½ tsp each turmeric, ground cumin & coriander/cilantro
1 tbsp medium curry powder
3 lemongrass stalks, finely chopped
5 curry leaves
200g/7oz spinach
2 tbsp tomato puree/paste
180ml/¾ cup vegetable stock/broth
120ml/½ cup low fat coconut milk
Salt & pepper to taste
Low cal cooking oil spray

Beef & Red Pepper Kofta Curry
Serves 4

Ingredients:

500g/1lb 2oz lean beef mince
2 garlic cloves, crushed
2 tbsp fresh breadcrumbs
½ tsp each ground turmeric, coriander/cilantro, paprika, ginger, brown sugar, garam masala & salt
1 red chilli, finely chopped
1 onion, sliced
3 red peppers, sliced
250ml/1 cup tomato passata/sieved tomatoes
60ml/¼ cup beef stock/broth
2 tbsp tomato puree/paste
Salt & pepper to taste
Low cal cooking oil spray

Method:

- Place the beef mince, garlic cloves & breadcrumbs in a food processor and pulse a few times until combined.
- Take the mixture out and form into small meatballs with your hands.
- Add all the other ingredients to the slow cooker and place the meatballs on top.

Combine well, cover and leave to cook on high for 4-5 hours or until the meatballs are cooked through.

- For side dish options see page 14

To make breadcrumbs, whizz a slice of bread in a food processor for a few seconds.

Marrakesh Lime & Lamb Curry
Serves 4

Method:

- Season the lamb and quickly brown for a couple of minutes in a frying pan with a little low cal oil.
- Remove from the heat and place in the slow cooker along with all the other ingredients.
Combine well, cover and leave to cook on low for 6-8 hours or until the lamb is tender and cooked through.

- For side dish options see page 14

Lean neck is a good cut of fillet to use for this curry.

Ingredients:

500g/1lb 2oz lean lamb fillet, cubed
2 onions, finely chopped
2 garlic cloves, crushed
400g/14oz fresh chopped tomatoes
Zest & juice of 1 lime
1 tsp each ground turmeric, coriander/cilantro, brown sugar & paprika
½ tsp each ground ginger & hot chilli powder
A pinch of ground cinnamon, nutmeg & salt
120ml/ ½ cup vegetable stock/broth
Salt & pepper to taste
Low cal cooking oil spray

St. Bart's Pork Curry
Serves 4

Ingredients:

500g/1lb 2oz pork tenderloin, cubed
2 onions, finely chopped
1 red pepper, sliced
3 garlic cloves, crushed
150g/5oz butternut squash flesh, chopped
3 black cardamom pods, crushed
½ tsp fenugreek seeds
1 tbsp mild curry powder
1 tsp thyme leaves
250ml/1 cup chicken stock/broth
120ml/½ cup low fat coconut milk
Salt & pepper to taste
Low cal cooking oil spray

Method:

- Season the pork and quickly brown for a couple of minutes in a frying pan with a little low cal oil.
- Remove from the heat and place in the slow cooker along with all the other ingredients except the coconut milk.
- Combine well, cover and leave to cook on low for 4-6 hours or until the pork is tender and cooked through. Add the coconut milk to the slow cooker. Gently stir through and serve.

- For side dish options see page 14

Pumpkin or sweet potato rather than butternut squash will work just as well in this curry.

Spiced Meatball Curry

Serves 4

Method:

- Place the mince, garlic cloves & breadcrumbs in a food processor and pulse for a few seconds until combined.
- Take the mixture out and form into small meatballs with your hands.
- Add all the other ingredients to the slow cooker and place the meatballs on top.

Combine well, cover and leave to cook on high for 3-5 hours or until the meatballs are cooked through and the cauliflower is tender.

- For side dish options see page 14

You could brown the meatballs first in a frying pan for a few minutes if you have the time.

Ingredients:

500g/1lb 2oz lean pork mince
2 garlic cloves, crushed
2 tbsp fresh breadcrumbs
½ tsp each ground turmeric, coriander/cilantro, paprika, ginger, brown sugar, mild curry powder, garam masala & salt
1 tsp brown sugar
2 red chillies, finely chopped
1 onion, sliced
1 head cauliflower split into florets
250ml/1 cup tomato passata/sieved tomatoes
60ml/¼ cup vegetable stock/broth
2 tbsp tomato puree/paste
Salt & pepper to taste
Low cal cooking oil spray

Hot Bamboo Shoot Beef Curry
Serves 4

Ingredients:

500g/1lb 2oz lean beef stewing steak, cubed
1 tbsp hot curry powder
1 tbsp tomato puree/paste
200g/7oz ready to use bamboo shoots
400g/14oz tinned chopped tomatoes
2 onions, sliced
3 garlic cloves, crushed
1 tbsp dried thyme
60ml/¼ cup beef stock/broth
1 tbsp coconut cream
Salt & pepper to taste
Low cal cooking oil spray

Method:

- Season the steak and quickly brown for a couple of minutes in a frying pan with a little low cal oil.
- Remove from the heat and place in the slow cooker along with all the other ingredients except the coconut cream.
- Combine well, cover and leave to cook on low for 6-8 hours or until the beef is tender and cooked through.
- Add the coconut cream to the slow cooker. Gently stir through and serve.

- For side dish options see page 14

You could add the bamboo shoots towards the end of cooking if you prefer a little crunch.

Lamb Jalfrezi
Serves 4

Method:

- Season the lamb and quickly brown for a couple of minutes in a frying pan with a little low cal oil.
- Remove from the heat and place in the slow cooker along with all the other ingredients. Combine well, cover and leave to cook on low for 5-7 hours or until the lamb is tender and cooked through.

- For side dish options see page 14

Jalfrezi is a very popular dish, which traditionally contains fresh green chillies.

Ingredients:

500g/1lb 2oz lean lamb fillet, cubed
1 onion, finely chopped
2 garlic cloves, crushed
4 green chillies, finely sliced lengthways
½ tsp each cumin, turmeric, paprika, garam masala, ground coriander/cilantro, ginger, cayenne pepper, brown sugar & salt
2 tbsp tomato puree/paste
400g/14oz tinned chopped tomatoes
60ml/¼ cup vegetable stock/broth
Salt & pepper to taste
Low cal cooking oil spray

Beef Madras
Serves 4

Ingredients:

500g/1lb 2oz lean beef stewing steak, cubed
2 onions, sliced
2 garlic cloves, crushed
1 tbsp hot curry powder
½ tsp each cumin, turmeric, ground coriander/cilantro, brown sugar & salt
3 tbsp tomato puree/paste
400g/14oz tinned chopped tomatoes
60ml/¼ cup beef stock/broth
2 tsp lemon juice
Salt & pepper to taste
Low cal cooking oil spray

Method:

- Season the beef and quickly brown for a couple of minutes in a frying pan with a little low cal oil.
- Remove from the heat and place in the slow cooker along with all the other ingredients. Combine well, cover and leave to cook on low for 5-7 hours or until the beef is tender and cooked through.

- For side dish options see page 14

Madras is a hot curry. Feel free to alter the spice to suit your own palate.

LOSE WEIGHT *FAST*

THE
SLOW COOKER
SPICE
GUY/CURRY
DIET
RECIPE BOOK

POULTRY DISHES

Fiery Chicken Curry
Serves 4

Ingredients:

500g/1lb 2oz skinless chicken breast meat, cubed
2 tbsp tomato puree/paste
2 onions, finely chopped
2 garlic cloves, crushed
200g/7oz potatoes, diced
120ml/½ cup chicken stock/broth
250ml/1 cup tomato passata/sieved tomatoes
½ tsp each ground ginger, coriander/cilantro, turmeric, salt & cumin
2 tsp hot chilli powder & brown sugar
Salt & pepper to taste
Low cal cooking oil spray

Method:

- Season the chicken and place in the slow cooker along with all the other ingredients. Combine well, cover and leave to cook on low for 6-7 hours or until the chicken is tender and cooked through.

- For side dish options see page 14

You could also use cayenne pepper rather than hot chilli powder for this recipe.

Chicken & Almond Curry

Serves 4

270 CALORIES PER SERVING

Method:

- Season the chicken and quickly brown for a couple of minutes in a frying pan with a little low cal oil.
- Remove from the heat and place in the slow cooker along with all the other ingredients except the Greek yoghurt.
- Combine well, cover and leave to cook on high for 3-5 hours or until the chicken is tender and cooked through. Add the yoghurt to the slow cooker. Gently stir through and serve.

- For side dish options see page 14

Ingredients:

500g/1lb 2oz skinless chicken breast meat, cubed
2 onions, finely chopped
2 garlic cloves, crushed
1 tsp turmeric
½ tsp each ground coriander/cilantro, cumin, paprika, mild chilli powder, ground ginger & salt
1 tbsp ground almonds
1 tbsp tomato puree/paste
180ml/¾ cup chicken stock/broth
120ml/½ cup fat free Greek yoghurt
Salt & pepper to taste
Low cal cooking oil spray

The almonds give this Korma style dish a lovely nutty taste.

Chicken & Soy Curry
Serves 4

Ingredients:

500g/1lb 2oz skinless chicken breast meat, cubed
2 onions, finely chopped
3 garlic cloves, crushed
½ tsp each turmeric, ground ginger, coriander/cilantro, cumin, paprika & chilli powder
2 tbsp tomato puree/paste
1 tsp brown sugar
120ml/½ cup chicken stock/broth
120ml/½ cup soy sauce
Salt & pepper to taste
Low cal cooking oil spray

Method:

- Season the chicken and quickly brown for a couple of minutes in a frying pan with a little low cal oil.
- Remove from the heat and place in the slow cooker along with all the other ingredients.
Combine well, cover and leave to cook on high for 2-4 hours or until the chicken is tender and cooked through.

- For side dish options see page 14

The distinctive flavour of soy sauce is known as 'umami' in Japanese, which means "pleasant savoury taste".

Rogan Josh
Serves 4

Method:

- Season the chicken and quickly brown for a couple of minutes in a frying pan with a little low cal oil.
- Remove from the heat and place in the slow cooker along with all the other ingredients.

Combine well, cover and leave to cook on high for 4-6 hours or until the chicken is tender and cooked through.

- For side dish options see page 14

Ingredients:

500g/1lb 2oz skinless chicken breast meat, cubed
4 onions, sliced
2 garlic cloves, crushed
400g/14oz tinned chopped tomatoes
1 tsp turmeric
½ tsp each garam masala, ground coriander/cilantro, cumin, paprika, hot chilli powder, ground ginger & salt
3 tbsp tomato puree/paste
200g/7oz potatoes, finely chopped
1 tsp brown sugar
60ml/¼ cup chicken stock/broth
Salt & pepper to taste
Low cal cooking oil spray

This curry should have a thick onion and tomato base. Leave to cook for a little longer if it needs thickening.

Chicken & Butternut Squash Curry
Serves 4

Ingredients:

500g/1lb 2oz skinless chicken breast meat, cubed
1 tbsp medium curry powder
2 tbsp tomato puree/paste
2 onions, sliced
2 garlic cloves, crushed
2 tsp dried basil
2 carrots, sliced into batons
150g/5oz butternut squash, diced
2 celery stalks, chopped
250ml/1 cup chicken stock/broth
Salt & pepper to taste
Low cal cooking oil spray

Method:

- Season the chicken and quickly brown for a couple of minutes in a frying pan with a little low cal oil.
- Remove from the heat and place in the slow cooker along with all the other ingredients.
- Combine well, cover and leave to cook on low for 5-7 hours or until the chicken is tender and cooked through.

- For side dish options see page 14

You could use sweet potato rather than butternut squash in this recipe if you prefer.

Sweet Potato & Chicken Curry
Serves 4

Method:

- Season the chicken and quickly brown for a couple of minutes in a frying pan with a little low cal oil.
- Remove from the heat and place in the slow cooker along with all the other ingredients except the coconut milk.
- Combine well, cover and leave to cook on high for 3-5 hours or until the chicken and sweet potatoes are tender and cooked through.
- Add the coconut milk to the slow cooker. Gently stir through and serve.

- For side dish options see page 14

Add a little more stock during cooking if the dish needs it.

Ingredients:

500g/1lb 2oz skinless chicken breast meat, cubed
1 onion, sliced
2 garlic cloves, crushed
½ tsp each turmeric, ground cumin, coriander/cilantro, mild chilli powder, ginger, paprika, salt & garam masala
200g/7oz sweet potatoes, cubed
200g/7oz peas
2 tbsp tomato puree/paste
180ml/ ¾ cup chicken stock/broth
120ml/½ cup low fat coconut milk
Salt & pepper to taste
Low cal cooking oil spray

Chicken Keema
Serves 4

280 CALORIES PER SERVING

Ingredients:

500g/1lb 2oz lean chicken or turkey mince
2 onions, sliced
2 garlic cloves, crushed
½ tsp each turmeric, ground cumin & coriander/cilantro
2 tsp hot curry powder
200g/7oz peas
2 tbsp tomato puree/paste
180ml/¾ cup chicken stock/broth
120ml/½ fat free Greek yoghurt
Salt & pepper to taste
Low cal cooking oil spray

Method:

- Season the mince and quickly brown for a couple of minutes in a frying pan with a little low cal oil.
- Remove from the heat and place in the slow cooker along with all the other ingredients except the yoghurt.
- Combine well, cover and leave to cook on high for 3-5 hours or until the mince is cooked through.
- Add the Greek yoghurt to the slow cooker. Gently stir through and serve.

- For side dish options see page 14

Frozen peas are fine to use for this recipe. Place them in a little boiling water for a minute or two to warm through before adding to the slow cooker.

Garam Masala Chicken Curry
Serves 4

Method:

- Season the chicken and place in the slow cooker along with all the other ingredients.
- Combine well, cover and leave to cook on low for 4-6 hours or until the chicken is tender and cooked through.

- For side dish options see page 14

Ingredients:

500g/1lb 2oz skinless chicken breast meat, cubed
2 tbsp tomato puree/paste
3 onions, sliced
1 green pepper, sliced
2 garlic cloves, crushed
120ml/½ cup chicken stock/broth
120ml/½ cup tomato passata/sieved tomatoes
2 tsp garam masala
½ tsp each ground coriander/cilantro, turmeric, hot chilli powder, ginger & cumin
2 tsp brown sugar
125g/4oz green beans, chopped
Salt & pepper to taste
Low cal cooking oil spray

Garam masala is a standard shop-bought spice in the west, however its components vary dramatically in Asia where regional variations are commonplace.

Chicken & Tamarind Curry
Serves 4

260 CALORIES PER SERVING

Ingredients:

500g/1lb 2oz skinless chicken breast meat, cubed
2 onions, sliced
2 garlic cloves, crushed
½ tsp each turmeric, ground cumin & coriander/cilantro
2 tsp medium curry powder
3 lemongrass stalks, finely chopped
2 tsp tamarind paste
Juice & zest of 1 lime
3 curry leaves
200g/7oz spinach
2 tbsp tomato puree/paste
120ml/½ cup vegetable stock/broth
120ml/½ cup low fat coconut milk
Salt & pepper to taste
Low cal cooking oil spray

Method:

- Season the chicken and place in the slow cooker along with all the other ingredients except the coconut milk.
- Combine well, cover and leave to cook on high for 3-5 hours or until the chicken is tender and cooked through.
- Add the coconut milk to the slow cooker. Gently stir through and serve.

- For side dish options see page 14

Additional lime wedges make a nice garnish for this dish.

Chicken & Mango Curry

Serves 4

Method:

- Season the chicken and place in the slow cooker along with all the other ingredients except the coconut milk.
- Combine well, cover and leave to cook on high for 3-5 hours or until the chicken and mangoes are tender and cooked through.
- Add the coconut milk to the slow cooker. Gently stir through and serve.

- For side dish options see page 14

Ripe mangos are fine to use in this dish. Add them an hour before the end of cooking time so that they don't lose their form.

Ingredients:

500g/1lb 2oz skinless chicken breast meat, cubed
2 onions, sliced
2 garlic cloves, crushed
½ tsp each turmeric, ground cumin & coriander/cilantro
2 tsp medium curry powder
2 tbsp tomato puree/paste
120ml/½ cup chicken stock/broth
120ml/½ cup low fat coconut milk
2 un-ripened mangos, peeled & de-stoned
Salt & pepper to taste
Low cal cooking oil spray

Thai Chicken Pieces
Serves 4

Ingredients:

500g/1lb 2oz skinless boneless chicken thighs
2 onions, finely chopped
3 tbsp Thai red curry paste
150g/5oz mushrooms, sliced
4 tbsp freshly chopped coriander/cilantro
1 red pepper, sliced
2 carrots, sliced into batons
250ml/1 cup chicken stock/broth
Salt & pepper to taste
Low cal cooking oil spray

Method:

- Season the chicken and place in the slow cooker along with all the other ingredients.
- Combine well, cover and leave to cook on high for 3-5 hours or until the chicken is tender and cooked through.

- For side dish options see page 14

Reserve a little chopped coriander for garnish.

Fresh Tomato & Basil Chicken Curry
Serves 4

Method:

- Season the chicken and place in the slow cooker along with all the other ingredients except the coconut cream.
- Combine well, cover and leave to cook on high for 3-5 hours or until the chicken is tender and cooked through.
- Add the coconut cream to the slow cooker. Gently stir through and serve.

- For side dish options see page 14

Ingredients:

500g/1lb 2oz skinless boneless chicken thighs, sliced
400g/14oz vine ripened chopped tomatoes
2 onions, sliced
3 garlic cloves, crushed
1 tbsp mild curry powder
2 tbsp tomato puree/paste
1 tsp brown sugar
½ tsp salt
4 tbsp freshly chopped basil
60ml/¼ cup chicken stock/broth
1 tbsp coconut cream
Salt & pepper to taste
Low cal cooking oil spray

Dried basil or oregano will also work well in this recipe.

'Butter' Chicken
Serves 4

Ingredients:

500g/1lb 2oz skinless chicken breast meat, cubed
2 tbsp low fat olive spread
2 garlic cloves, crushed
½ tsp each ground turmeric, cumin, coriander/cilantro, paprika, ginger, crushed chilli flakes, garam masala & salt
1 tsp brown sugar
250ml/1 cup tomato passata/sieved tomatoes
60ml/¼ cup vegetable stock/broth
3 tbsp tomato puree/paste
120ml/½ cup fat free Greek yoghurt
Salt & pepper to taste
Low cal cooking oil spray

Method:

- Season the chicken and seal for a couple of minutes in a frying pan with a little low cal oil.
- Remove from the heat and place in the slow cooker along with all the other ingredients except the yoghurt.
- Combine well, cover and leave to cook on high for 3-5 hours or until the chicken is tender and cooked through.
- Add the yoghurt to the slow cooker. Gently stir through and serve.

- For side dish options see page 14

This is a great 'skinny' version of the classic calorific dish.

Chicken Bhuna
Serves 4

Method:

- Season the chicken and quickly brown for a couple of minutes in a frying pan with a little low cal oil.
- Remove from the heat and place in the slow cooker along with all the other ingredients except the Greek yoghurt.
- Combine well, cover and leave to cook on high for 3-5 hours or until the chicken is tender and cooked through.
- Add the yoghurt to the slow cooker. Gently stir through and serve.

- For side dish options see page 14

Use any mixture of vegetables you prefer for this classic medium dish.

Ingredients:

500g/1lb 2oz skinless chicken breast meat, cubed
1 onion, finely chopped
250g/9oz mixture of chopped carrots, cauliflower & peas
2 garlic cloves, crushed
½ tsp each cumin, turmeric, paprika, garam masala, medium chilli powder, ground coriander/cilantro, brown sugar & salt
A pinch of cardamom and fenugreek seeds
2 tbsp tomato puree/paste
400g/14oz tinned chopped tomatoes
60ml/ ¼ cup chicken stock/broth
1 tbsp fat free Greek yoghurt
Salt & pepper to taste
Low cal cooking oil spray

Chicken Dopiaza
Serves 4

Ingredients:

500g/1lb 2oz skinless chicken breast meat, cubed
4 onions, thickly sliced
2 garlic cloves, crushed
½ tsp each cumin, turmeric, paprika, garam masala, hot chilli powder, ground coriander/cilantro, ginger, brown sugar & salt
2 tbsp tomato puree/paste
180/¾ cup tomato passata/sieved tomatoes
60ml/¼ cup chicken stock/broth
Salt & pepper to taste
Low cal cooking oil spray

Method:

- Season the chicken and quickly brown for a couple of minutes in a frying pan with a little low cal oil.
- Remove from the heat and place in the slow cooker along with all the other ingredients.
- Combine well, cover and leave to cook on high for 3-5 hours or until the chicken is tender and cooked through.

- For side dish options see page 14

Onions and a thick sauce are the calling cards of this curry.

Garlic Chicken
Serves 4

Method:

- Season the chicken and gently sauté for a couple of minutes in a frying pan with a little low cal oil and the sliced garlic.
- Remove from the heat and place in the slow cooker along with all the other ingredients.
- Combine well, cover and leave to cook on high for 3-5 hours or until the chicken is tender and cooked through.

- For side dish options see page 14

Ingredients:

500g/1lb 2oz skinless chicken breast meat, cubed
14 garlic cloves, peeled & finely sliced
1 onion, chopped
½ tsp each cumin, turmeric, paprika, garam masala, hot chilli powder, ground coriander/cilantro, brown sugar & salt
1 tbsp tomato puree/paste
2 vine ripened tomatoes, roughly chopped
180ml/¾ cup tomato passata/sieved tomatoes
60ml/¼ cup chicken stock/broth
Salt & pepper to taste
Low cal cooking oil spray

Be careful not to burn the garlic when you sauté with the chicken. A few drops if water in the pan can help prevent this.

Chicken Korma
Serves 4

Ingredients:

500g/1lb 2oz skinless chicken breast meat, cubed
2 garlic cloves, crushed
1 onion, chopped
2 tsp mild curry powder
½ tsp each cumin, turmeric, paprika & salt
2 tbsp tomato puree/paste
250ml/1 cup tomato passata/sieved tomatoes
60ml/¼ cup low fat coconut milk
1 tbsp ground almonds
Salt & pepper to taste
Low cal cooking oil spray

Method:

- Season the chicken and quickly brown for a couple of minutes in a frying pan with a little low cal oil.
- Remove from the heat and place in the slow cooker along with all the other ingredients except the coconut milk & ground almonds.
- Combine well, cover and leave to cook on high for 3-5 hours or until the chicken is tender and cooked through.
- Add the coconut milk to the slow cooker. Gently stir through and serve with the ground almonds sprinkled over the top.

- For side dish options see page 14

Korma dishes are traditionally 'nutty'. This version contains both coconut milk and ground almonds.

Tandoori Chicken
Serves 4

Method:

- Mix together all the ingredients, except the chicken, to form a yoghurt paste.
- Season the chicken and smother with the yoghurt paste.
- Place in the slow cooker, cover and leave to cook on high for 2-4 hours or until the chicken is tender and cooked through.

- For side dish options see page 14

This dish is great served with a simple green salad.

Ingredients:

12 chicken drumsticks
Juice and zest from 1 lemon
2 garlic cloves, crushed
1 tbsp tomato puree/paste
1 tsp mild chilli powder
½ tsp each salt, cumin, turmeric, paprika & black pepper
250ml/1 cup fat free Greek yoghurt
Salt & pepper to taste
Low cal cooking oil spray

Simple Creamy Chicken Curry
Serves 4

Ingredients:

500g/1lb 2oz skinless chicken breast meat, cubed
2 tbsp tomato puree/paste
1 onion, finely chopped
2 garlic cloves, crushed
2 tsp mild curry powder
½ tsp each ground coriander/cilantro, turmeric & cumin
1 tsp brown sugar
120ml/½ cup tomato passata/sieved tomatoes
60ml/ ½ cup chicken stock/broth
60ml/ ½ cup low fat crème fraiche
Salt & pepper to taste
Low cal cooking oil spray

Method:

- Season the chicken and place in the slow cooker along with all the other ingredients except the crème fraiche.
- Combine well, cover and leave to cook on high for 3-5 hours or until the chicken is tender and cooked through.
- Stir through the crème fraiche and serve.

- For side dish options see page 14

This is a really simple, mild curry which should suit everyone's palate.

Dhansak
Serves 4

Method:

- Season the chicken and quickly brown for a couple of minutes in a frying pan with a little low cal oil.
- Remove from the heat and place in the slow cooker along with all the other ingredients except the pineapple chunks.
- Combine well, cover and leave to cook on high for 3-5 hours or until the chicken is tender and cooked through.
- 45 minutes before the end of cooking add the pineapple chunks to the slow cooker.
- Season and serve.

- For side dish options see page 14

You could also use fresh pineapple for this dish if you prefer.

Ingredients:

500g/1lb 2oz skinless chicken breast meat, cubed
2 onions, chopped
2 garlic cloves, crushed
½ tsp each cumin, turmeric, paprika, garam masala, ground coriander/cilantro, ginger, brown sugar & salt
2 tbsp tomato puree/paste
250ml/1 cup tomato passata/sieved tomatoes
60ml/ ¼ cup chicken stock/broth
125g/4oz pineapple chunks, chopped
Salt & pepper to taste
Low cal cooking oil spray

Chicken Pasanda
Serves 4

Ingredients:

500g/1lb 2oz skinless chicken breast meat, cubed
2 garlic cloves, crushed
1 onion, chopped
1 tbsp mild curry powder
½ tsp salt & brown sugar
3 tbsp tomato puree/paste
250ml/1 cup tomato passata/sieved tomatoes
60ml/¼ cup chicken stock/broth
60ml/¼ cup fat free Greek yoghurt
2 tbsp chopped cashew nuts
Salt & pepper to taste
Low cal cooking oil spray

Method:

- Season the chicken and quickly brown for a couple of minutes in a frying pan with a little low cal oil.
- Remove from the heat and place in the slow cooker along with all the other ingredients except the yoghurt & cashew nuts. Combine well, cover and leave to cock on high for 3-5 hours or until the chicken is tender and cooked through.
- Meanwhile gently toast the chopped cashew nuts in the frying pan with a little low cal oil for 2-3 minutes until they begin to brown and become fragrant.
- When the chicken is ready add the Greek yoghurt to the slow cooker. Gently stir through and serve with the toasted cashew nuts sprinkled over the top.

- For side dish options see page 14

Toasted almonds also work well for this dish in place of cashew nuts.

Chicken & Split Pea Curry
Serves 4

Method:

- Place all the ingredients in the slow cooker.
- Combine well, cover and leave to cook on low for 6-8 hours or until the peas & chicken are tender and cooked through.

- For side dish options see page 14

Add a little more stock during cooking if the dish needs it.

Ingredients:

500g/1lb 2oz skinless chicken breast meat, cubed
150g/5oz pre soaked split peas
1 tbsp medium curry powder
½ tsp each ground cumin, mustard seeds, salt & brown sugar
2 tbsp tomato puree/paste
370ml/1 ½ cups chicken stock/broth
2 tbsp coconut cream
Salt & pepper to taste
Low cal cooking oil spray

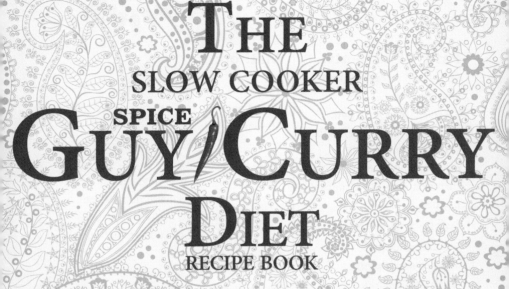

THE SLOW COOKER SPICE GUY/CURRY DIET
RECIPE BOOK

SEAFOOD DISHES

King Prawn Masala
Serves 4

Paste Ingredients:
500g/1lb 2oz raw shelled king prawns
2 garlic cloves, crushed
1 tbsp tomato puree/paste
½ tsp each mild chilli powder, salt, cumin, turmeric, paprika & black pepper

Paste Ingredients:
1 onion, chopped
1 tsp cayenne pepper
½ tsp each cumin, turmeric, paprika, garam masala, ground coriander/cilantro & brown sugar & salt
2 tbsp tomato puree/paste
3 vine ripened tomatoes, roughly chopped
180ml/¾ cup tomato passata/sieved tomatoes
60ml/¼ cup chicken stock/broth
120ml/½ cup fat free Greek yoghurt
Lemon wedges to serve
Salt & pepper to taste
Low cal cooking oil spray

Method:
- First mix together the paste ingredients and rub into the king prawns.
- Cover and leave to marinade in a bowl.
- Meanwhile place all the sauce ingredients, except the lemon wedges and Greek yoghurt, in the slow cooker.
- Cover and leave to cook on high for 2 hours.
- Add the prawns and cook for a further 40-70 minutes or until the prawns are cooked through.
- Add the Greek yoghurt and serve with the lemon wedges.

- For side dish options see page 14

Reduce the cayenne pepper in the sauce if your find this dish too spicy for your taste.

King Prawn & Fresh Pea Curry
Serves 4

Method:

- Place all the ingredients in the slow cooker, except the coconut milk.
- Combine well, cover and leave to cook on high for 3-5 hours or until the prawns are cooked through.
- Add the coconut milk to the slow cooker. Gently stir through and serve.
- For side dish options see page 14

You could hold off adding the fresh peas until 30 mins before the end of cooking if you want them to have a little crunch.

Ingredients:

500g/1lb 2oz raw king prawns
200g/7oz fresh peas
200g/7oz vine ripened tomatoes, roughly chopped
2 garlic cloves, crushed
1 onion, chopped
½ tsp each turmeric, cayenne pepper, cumin, coriander/cilantro, paprika, salt & brown sugar
2 tbsp tomato puree/paste
120ml/½ cup tomato passata/sieved tomatoes
120ml/½ cup low fat coconut milk
Salt & pepper to taste
Low cal cooking oil spray

Paka Hua Alu
Serves 4

Ingredients:

500g/1lb 2oz scallops
150g/5oz spinach
2 garlic cloves, crushed
1 green chilli, finely chopped
1 onion, sliced
250g/9oz vine ripened tomatoes, roughly chopped
½ tsp ground ginger
1 tbsp mild curry powder
60ml/¼ cup fish stock/ broth
120ml/½ cup low fat crème fraiche
Salt & pepper to taste
Low cal cooking oil spray

Method:

- Place all the ingredients in the slow cooker, except the crème fraiche.
- Combine well, cover and leave to cook on high for 1-3 hours or until the scallops are cooked through.
- Add the crème fraiche, stir & serve.

- For side dish options see page 14

Paka Hua Alu is is the Hindi word for scallops. The fresher the scallops are the better this dish will taste.

Thai Fish Curry
Serves 4

Method:

- Place all the ingredients in the slow cooker, except the coconut milk.
- Combine well, cover and leave to cook on high for 1-3 hours or until the fish is cooked through.
- Add the coconut milk and combine well.

- For side dish options see page 14

Ingredients:

500g/1lb 2oz firm white fish fillets, cubed
2 garlic cloves, crushed
½ red chilli, finely chopped
2 onions, sliced
Zest and juice of ½ lime
3 tbsp Thai green curry paste
½ tsp ground coriander/cilantro
120ml/½ cup chicken stock/broth
60ml/¼ cup low fat coconut milk
Salt & pepper to taste
Low cal cooking oil spray

Any type of firm white fish will work for this dish. Ensure the bones and skin are removed.

Ginger & Fresh Tomato Prawns
Serves 4

Ingredients:

500g/1lb 2oz raw, shelled king prawns
2 tsp freshly grated ginger
½ tsp each turmeric, cumin, coriander/cilantro, paprika, salt & brown sugar
1 red chilli, thinly sliced
200g/7oz vine ripened tomatoes, roughly chopped
2 garlic cloves, crushed
1 onion, sliced
2 tbsp tomato puree/paste
Salt & pepper to taste
Low cal cooking oil spray

Method:

- Mix the prawns, fresh ginger and turmeric together until the prawns are well covered.
- Place all the ingredients in the slow cooker. Combine well, cover and leave to cook on high for 1-3 hours or until the prawns are cooked through.

- For side dish options see page 14

If you don't have fresh ginger use a tsp ground ginger instead.

Mackerel Curry
Serves 4

Method:

- Place all the ingredients in the slow cooker.
- Combine well, cover and leave to cook on high for 1-3 hours or until the fish is cooked through.

- For side dish options see page 14

Ingredients:

500g/1lb 2oz skinless, boneless mackerel fillets
2 garlic cloves, crushed
2 onions, sliced
1 tsp freshly grated ginger
1 tsp cumin seeds
1 tbsp medium curry powder
400g/14oz tinned chopped tomatoes
½ tsp salt & brown sugar
2 tbsp tomato puree/paste
½ red chilli, sliced
Salt & pepper to taste
Low cal cooking oil spray

Mackerel a lovely oily fish which is a rich source of essential omega-3 fatty acids.

Coconut Milk & Fish Curry
Serves 4

Ingredients:

500g/1lb 2oz firm white fish fillets, cubed
½ tsp each ground cumin, turmeric & coriander/cilantro
2 garlic cloves, crushed
2 red chillies, sliced lengthways
1 onion, sliced
250ml/1 cup low fat coconut milk
2 tbsp freshly chopped coriander/cilantro
Salt & pepper to taste
Low cal cooking oil spray

Method:

- Place all the ingredients in the slow cooker, except the chopped coriander.
- Combine well, cover and leave to cook on high for 1-3 hours or until the fish is cooked through.
- Sprinkle with chopped coriander and serve.

- For side dish options see page 14

Sliced spring onions also make a lovely additional garnish for this dish.

Pineapple & Prawn Curry
Serves 4

Method:

- Place all the ingredients in the slow cooker.
- Combine well, cover and leave to cook on high for 1-3 hours or until the prawns are cooked through.
- or side dish options see page 14

Ingredients:

500g/1lb 2oz raw, shelled king prawns
½ tsp each turmeric, brown sugar & salt
1 tbsp medium curry powder
2 tsp each fish sauce & tamarind paste
200g/7oz tinned pineapple, chopped
1 lemongrass stalk, finely chopped
2 garlic cloves, crushed
1 onion, chopped
2 tbsp tomato puree/paste
120ml/½ cup low fat coconut milk
Salt & pepper to taste
Low cal cooking oil spray

The pineapple and tamarind combine well to give a lovely sweet & sour taste.

Fresh Mussel Curry
Serves 4

Ingredients:

1.kg/3lb 6oz fresh cleaned mussels
2 garlic cloves, crushed
1 onion, chopped
1 tbsp mild curry powder
½ tsp each cumin, turmeric, paprika & salt
2 tbsp tomato puree/paste
250ml/1 cup tomato passata/sieved tomatoes
60ml/¼ cup low fat coconut milk
3 tbsp freshly chopped flat leaf parsley
Salt & pepper to taste
Low cal cooking oil spray

Method:

- Place all the ingredients in the slow cooker, except the chopped parsley.
- Combine well, cover and leave to cook on high for 2-4 hours or until the mussels have opened (discard any which do not open).
- Stir well, sprinkle with parsley and serve in shallow bowls.

- For side dish options see page 14

Buy the freshest mussels possible to get the best result from this dish.

THE SLOW COOKER SPICE GUY/CURRY DIET RECIPE BOOK

LOSE WEIGHT FAST

RECIPE BOOK

VEGETABLE CURRIES

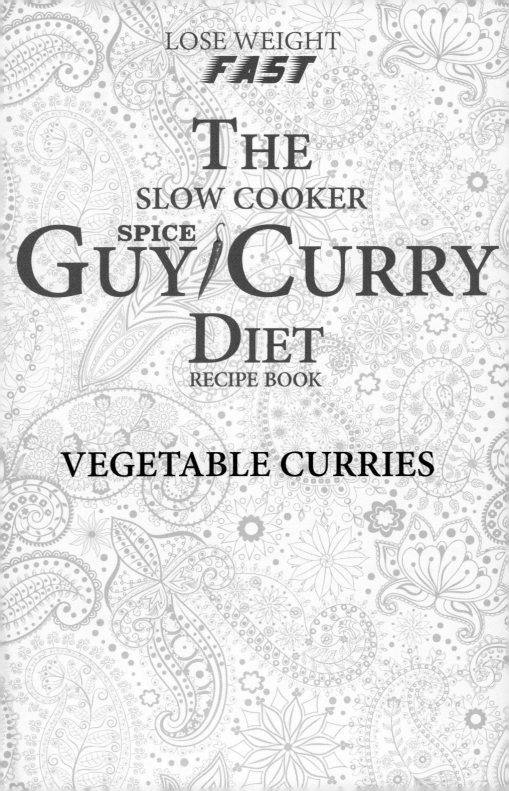

Aloo Gobi
Serves 4

Ingredients:

1 large cauliflower head, split into florets
½ green cabbage, shredded
200g/7oz potatoes, cubed
400g/14oz tinned chopped tomatoes
2 garlic cloves, crushed
1 onion, chopped
1 tsp turmeric
½ tsp each cayenne pepper, cumin, coriander/cilantro, paprika, garam masala, salt & brown sugar
2 tbsp tomato puree/paste
60ml/¼ cup vegetable stock/broth
2 tbsp chopped coriander/cilantro
Salt & pepper to taste
Low cal cooking oil spray

Method:

- Place all the ingredients in the slow cooker, except the chopped coriander.
- Combine well, cover and leave to cook on high for 3-5 hours or until the vegetables are tender and cooked through.
- Sprinkle with chopped coriander and serve.

- For side dish options see page 14

Spinach and broccoli make good additions to this dish too.

Simple Vegetable Curry

Serves 4

170 CALORIES PER SERVING

Method:

- Place all the ingredients in the slow cooker.
- Combine well, cover and leave to cook on high for 3-5 hours or until the vegetables are tender and cooked through.

- For side dish options see page 14

Add some fresh sliced chillies as a garnish if you want to introduce a little more 'bite' to this dish.

Ingredients:

2 carrots cut into batons
1 large cauliflower head, split into florets
200g/7oz spinach leaves
125g/4oz peas
2 onions, chopped
400g/14oz tinned chopped tomatoes
2 garlic cloves, crushed
1 tbsp mild curry powder
½ tsp each salt & brown sugar
2 tbsp tomato puree/paste
60ml/¼ cup vegetable stock/broth
Salt & pepper to taste
Low cal cooking oil spray

Saag Aloo
Serves 4

Ingredients:

400g/14oz spinach leaves
½ green cabbage, shredded
200g/7oz potatoes, cubed
2 garlic cloves, crushed
1 onion, chopped
½ tsp each turmeric, ginger, cumin, coriander/cilantro, paprika & mustard seeds
120ml/ ½ cup vegetable stock/broth
2 tbsp freshly chopped coriander/cilantro
Lemon wedges to serve
Salt & pepper to taste
Low cal cooking oil spray

Method:

- Place all the ingredients in the slow cooker, except the chopped coriander & lemon wedges.
- Combine well, cover and leave to cook on high for 3-5 hours or until the vegetables are tender and cooked through.
- Sprinkle with chopped coriander, place the lemon wedges on the side and serve.

- For side dish options see page 14

If you have time, you could first quickly sauté the mustard seeds in a little low cal oil for a minute or two until they begin to pop.

Masaruma & Tomato Curry
Serves 4

Method:

- Place all the ingredients in the slow cooker, except the coconut milk.
- Combine well, cover and leave to cook on high for 3-5 hours or until the vegetables are tender and cooked through.
- Add the coconut milk to the slow cooker. Gently stir through and serve.

- For side dish options see page 14

Ingredients:

500g/1lb 2oz mixed mushrooms, halved
200g/7oz vine ripened tomatoes, roughly chopped
2 garlic cloves, crushed
1 onion, chopped
1 tsp each turmeric, mild chilli powder, cumin, coriander/cilantro, paprika, salt & brown sugar
1 tbsp tomato puree/paste
250ml/1 cup tomato passata/sieved tomatoes
60ml/¼ cup low fat coconut milk
Salt & pepper to taste
Low cal cooking oil spray

If you choose to use large flat mushrooms for this dish they will need to be thickly sliced rather than halved.

Broccoli & Mini Corn Curry
Serves 4

Ingredients:

200g/1lb 2oz tenderstem broccoli, halved lengthways
200g/7oz fresh mini corn, left whole
3 carrots, sliced into batons
200g/7oz vine ripened tomatoes, roughly chopped
2 garlic cloves, crushed
1 onion, chopped
½ tsp each turmeric, mild chilli powder, cumin, coriander/cilantro, brown sugar, paprika & salt
2 tbsp tomato puree/paste
120ml/ ½ cup tomato passata/sieved tomatoes
60ml/¼ cup vegetable stock
Salt & pepper to taste
Low cal cooking oil spray

Method:

- Place all the ingredients in the slow cooker.
- Combine well, cover and leave to cook on high for 3-5 hours or until the vegetables are tender and cooked through.

- For side dish options see page 14

Tenderstem broccoli is a lovely seasonal ingredient; use regular fresh broccoli florets if they aren't available.

Thai Squash & Coconut Curry
Serves 4

Method:

- Place all the ingredients in the slow cooker, except the coconut milk and lime wedges.
- Combine well, cover and leave to cook on high for 3-5 hours or until the vegetables are tender and cooked through.
- Add the coconut milk to the slow cooker.
- Gently stir through and serve with the lime wedges.

Ingredients:

500g/1lb 2oz butternut squash flesh, cubed
2 onions, finely chopped
3 tbsp Thai red curry paste
½ tsp ground coriander/cilantro
2 carrots, sliced into batons
120ml/½ cup vegetable stock/broth
120ml/½ cup low fat coconut milk
Limes wedges to serve
Salt & pepper to taste
Low cal cooking oil spray

- For side dish options see page 14

Make sure this dish doesn't dry out by adding a little more stock during cooking if needed.

Coriander & Sweet Potato Curry
Serves 4

Ingredients:

500g/1lb 2oz sweet potatoes, cubed
2 onions, finely chopped
½ tsp each turmeric, mild chilli powder, cumin, coriander/cilantro, paprika & salt
1 red chilli, finely chopped
2 carrots, sliced into batons
120ml/½ cup vegetable stock/broth
120ml/½ cup low fat coconut milk
2 tbsp freshly chopped coriander/cilantro
Lime wedges to serve
Salt & pepper to taste
Low cal cooking oil spray

Method:

- Place all the ingredients in the slow cooker, except the coconut milk, chopped coriander & lime wedges.
- Combine well, cover and leave to cook on high for 3-5 hours or until the vegetables are tender and cooked through.
- Add the coconut milk to the slow cooker. Gently stir through, sprinkle with chopped coriander and serve with the lime wedges.

- For side dish options see page 14

Sweet potatoes are a fantastic versatile vegetable, which form the base of many Caribbean curries.

Spinach & Paneer
Serves 4

Method:

- Place all the ingredients in the slow cooker, except the crème fraiche & chopped coriander.
- Combine well, cover and leave to cook on high for 3-5 hours or until everything is tender and cooked through.
- Add the crème fraiche to the slow cooker. Gently stir through, sprinkle with chopped coriander and serve.

- For side dish options see page 14

Ingredients:

400g/14oz spinach leaves
200g/7oz paneer
200g/7oz vine ripened tomatoes, roughly chopped
2 garlic cloves, crushed
1 onion, chopped
1 tsp each turmeric, cumin, coriander/cilantro, paprika & mustard seeds
½ tsp ground ginger & cayenne pepper
Juice of ½ lemon
60ml/¼ cup vegetable stock/broth
60ml/¼ cup crème fraiche
2 tbsp freshly chopped coriander/cilantro
Salt & pepper to taste
Low cal cooking oil spray

Paneer is the Indian version of cottage cheese, which is now widely available in the UK & US.

Cumin & Spinach Potatoes
Serves 4

Ingredients:

400g/14oz potatoes, cubed
200g/7oz spinach
1 tsp each ground cumin, coriander/cilantro & mustard seeds
½ tsp salt
½ green cabbage, shredded
120ml/½ cup vegetable stock/broth
2 tbsp freshly chopped coriander/cilantro
Lemon wedges to serve
Salt & pepper to taste
Low cal cooking oil spray

Method:

- Place all the ingredients in the slow cooker except the chopped coriander and lime wedges.
- Combine well, cover and leave to cook on high for 3-5 hours or until the potatoes are tender and cooked through.
- Sprinkle with chopped coriander and serve with the lemon wedges.

- For side dish options see page 14

Pointed cabbage rather than savoy cabbage will work best in this recipe.

260 CALORIES PER SERVING

Egg Curry
Serves 4

Method:

- Place all the ingredients in the slow cooker, except the coconut milk and eggs.
- Combine well, cover and leave to cook on high for 2 hours.
- Add the boiled eggs and leave to warm through for 30-40 mins.
- Add the coconut milk, combine well and serve.

- For side dish options see page 14

Ingredients:

2 garlic cloves, crushed
2 onions, chopped
2 tsp mild curry powder
½ tsp each cumin, turmeric, paprika & salt
2 tbsp tomato puree/paste
250ml/1 cup tomato passata/sieved tomatoes
8 hardboiled peeled eggs, halved
120ml/½ cup low fat coconut milk
Salt & pepper to taste
Low cal cooking oil spray

Egg curries are a very popular main course in India. Use organic eggs for the best yolks.

Chickpea Curry
Serves 4

Ingredients:

600g/1lb 9oz tinned chickpeas, drained
200g/7oz spinach
2 tsp medium curry powder
½ tsp ground cumin, mustard seeds, salt & brown sugar
2 tbsp tomato puree/paste
250ml/1 cup vegetable stock/broth
Salt & pepper to taste
Low cal cooking oil spray

Method:

- Place all the ingredients in the slow cooker.
- Combine well, cover and leave to cook on high for 2-4 hours or until the chickpeas are cooked through.

- For side dish options see page 14

Dried chickpeas are fine to use if they are pre-soaked and prepared.

240 CALORIES PER SERVING

Red Lentil & Courgette Curry
Serves 4

Method:

- Place all the ingredients in the slow cooker.
- Combine well, cover and leave to cook on low for 6-8 hours or until the lentils are tender and cooked through.

- For side dish options see page 14

Ingredients:

300g/11oz courgettes/zucchini thickly sliced
150g/5oz red lentils
2 tsp medium curry powder
½ tsp ground coriander/cilantro, cumin, mustard seeds, salt & brown sugar
2 tbsp tomato puree/paste
200g/7oz tinned chopped tomatoes
120ml/½ cup vegetable stock/broth
Salt & pepper to taste
Low cal cooking oil spray

Add a little more stock during cooking if the lentils require it.

Munga Curry
Serves 4

Ingredients:

600g/1lb 9oz tinned kidney beans
200g/7oz green beans
1 onion, chopped
2 garlic cloves, crushed
½ tsp each ground coriander/cilantro, mild chilli powder, turmeric, cumin, garam masala & salt
120ml/½ cup vegetable stock/broth
60ml/¼ cup crème fraiche
Salt & pepper to taste
Low cal cooking oil spray

Method:

- Place all the ingredients in the slow cooker.
- Combine well, cover and leave to cook on high for 2-4 hours or until the kidney beans are cooked through.

- For side dish options see page 14

Munga is the Hindi word for kidney beans.

270 CALORIES PER SERVING

Onion & Egg Masala
Serves 4

Method:

- Place all the ingredients in the slow cooker, except the Greek yoghurt and eggs.
- Combine well, cover and leave to cook on high for 3-4 hours.
- Add the boiled eggs, stir and leave to warm through for 30-40 mins.
- Add the yoghurt, combine well and serve.

- For side dish options see page 14

Ingredients:

4 onions, sliced
½ tsp each cumin, turmeric, paprika, garam masala, cayenne pepper, ground coriander/cilantro, brown sugar, ginger & salt
2 tbsp tomato puree/paste
3 vine ripened tomatoes, roughly chopped
250ml/1 cup tomato passata/sieved tomatoes
60ml/¼ cup chicken stock/broth
4 hardboiled eggs, peeled & halved
120ml/½ cup fat free Greek yoghurt
Salt & pepper to taste
Low cal cooking oil spray

Slice the onions thickly to give the curry a robust base.

Aloo Cauliflower Curry
Serves 4

Ingredients:

1 large cauliflower heads, split into florets
1 green pepper, sliced
125g/4oz peas
1 onion, chopped
200g/7oz tinned chopped tomatoes
2 garlic cloves, crushed
½ tsp each turmeric, cayenne pepper, cumin, coriander/cilantro & paprika
1 tbsp tomato puree/paste
60ml/¼ cup vegetable stock/broth
4 tbsp freshly chopped flat leaf parsley
Salt & pepper to taste
Low cal cooking oil spray

Method:

- Place all the ingredients in the slow cooker.
- Combine well, cover and leave to cook on high for 3-5 hours or until the vegetables are tender and cooked through.

- For side dish options see page 14

Hold back a little of the parsley as a garnish.

210 CALORIES PER SERVING

Plantain & Sweet Onion Curry
Serves 4

Method:

- Place all the ingredients in the slow cooker, except the coconut milk.
- Combine well, cover and leave to cook on high for 3-5 hours or until the plantain is tender and cooked through.
- Add the coconut milk, stir and serve.

Ingredients:

2 plantain, peeled & thickly sliced
250g/9oz shallots, halved
2 tsp mild curry powder
½ tsp each cumin, turmeric, paprika, salt, ground cinnamon & brown sugar
2 tbsp tomato puree/paste
125g/4oz vine ripened tomatoes, roughly chopped
120ml/ ½ cup vegetable stock/broth
120ml/½ cup low fat coconut milk
Salt & pepper to taste
Low cal cooking oil spray

- For side dish options see page 14

Plantain is a West Indian vegetable, which is now widely available in the UK & US.

Garlic Curry
Serves 4

Ingredients:

1 whole bulb garlic, separated & peeled
2 green chillies, finely chopped
2 tsp tamarind paste
150g/5oz tenderstem broccoli
2 onions, roughly chopped
5 curry leaves
½ tsp each fennel seeds, turmeric, cayenne pepper, salt & brown sugar
2 tbsp tomato puree/paste
125g/4oz vine ripened tomatoes, roughly chopped
120ml/½ cup vegetable stock/broth
120ml/½ cup low fat crème fraiche
Salt & pepper to taste
Low cal cooking oil spray

Method:

- Place all the ingredients in the slow cooker, except the crème fraiche.
- Combine well, cover and leave to cook on high for 4-6 hours.
- Add the crème fraiche and combine well.
- Remove the curry leaves and serve.

- For side dish options see page 14

This curry is great served with a simple green salad.

Gobhi Coconut Curry
Serves 4

Method:

- Place all the ingredients in the slow cooker, except the desiccated coconut.
- Combine well, cover and leave to cook on high for 3-5 hours or until the vegetables are tender and cooked through.
- Meanwhile heat a dry frying pan and toast the coconut gently until golden brown.
- When the cabbage is ready, sprinkle with the toasted coconut and serve.

Ingredients:

1 large pointed green cabbage, shredded
1 green pepper, thinly sliced
2 green chillies, finely chopped
2 onions, thinly sliced
½ tsp each mustard seeds, turmeric & cumin
250ml/1 cup vegetable stock/broth
75g/3oz desiccated coconut
Salt & pepper to taste
Low cal cooking oil spray

- For side dish options see page 14

Shake the pan continuously to move the coconut around when you are toasting it.

Green Beans & Fenugreek Curry
Serves 4

Ingredients:

400g/14oz green beans, trimmed & split lengthways
1 red pepper, chopped
2 red chillies, finely chopped
2 onions, thinly sliced
½ tsp each fenugreek seeds, salt & turmeric
120ml/ ½ cup vegetable stock/broth
60ml/¼ cup coconut cream
Lime wedges to serve
Salt & pepper to taste
Low cal cooking oil spray

Method:

- Place all the ingredients in the slow cooker, except the coconut cream and lime wedges.
- Combine well, cover and leave to cook on high for 2-4 hours or until the beans are tender and cooked through.
- Add the coconut cream, stir & serve with the lime wedges.

- For side dish options see page 14

Widely used in Indian cooking, fenugreek seeds are believed to help fend off the common cold!

Cauliflower 'Rice'
Serves 4

Method:

- Split the cauliflower head into florets and place in a food processor.
- Whizz until the cauliflower is the size of rice grains.
- Place the 'rice' in a microwavable dish and cook covered for 4-5 minutes or until the 'rice' is piping hot.

Ingredients:

1 large cauliflower head (approx. 800g)

This is a great alternative to rice if you are trying to keep the calories down. It freezes well too, so make a batch and freeze into portions.

CONVERSION CHART: DRY INGREDIENTS

Metric	Imperial
7g	¼ oz
15g	½ oz
20g	¾ oz
25g	1 oz
40g	1½oz
50g	2oz
60g	2½oz
75g	3oz
100g	3½oz
125g	4oz
140g	4½oz
150g	5oz
165g	5½oz
175g	6oz
200g	7oz
225g	8oz
250g	9oz
275g	10oz
300g	11oz
350g	12oz
375g	13oz
400g	14oz

Metric	Imperial
425g	15oz
450g	1lb
500g	1lb 2oz
550g	1¼lb
600g	1lb 5oz
650g	1lb 7oz
675g	1½lb
700g	1lb 9oz
750g	1lb 11oz
800g	1¾lb
900g	2lb
1kg	2¼lb
1.1kg	2½lb
1.25kg	2¾lb
1.35kg	3lb
1.5kg	3lb 6oz
1.8kg	4lb
2kg	4½lb
2.25kg	5lb
2.5kg	5½lb
2.75kg	6lb

CONVERSION CHART: LIQUID MEASURES

Metric	Imperial	US
25ml	1fl oz	
60ml	2fl oz	¼ cup
75ml	2½ fl oz	
100ml	3½fl oz	
120ml	4fl oz	½ cup
150ml	5fl oz	
175ml	6fl oz	
200ml	7fl oz	
250ml	8½ fl oz	1 cup
300ml	10½ fl oz	
360ml	12½ fl oz	
400ml	14fl oz	
450ml	15½ fl oz	
600ml	1 pint	
750ml	1¼ pint	3 cups
1 litre	1½ pints	4 cups

Also Available

LOSE WEIGHT FOR GOOD

SLOW COOKER DIET
FOR BEGINNERS

CALORIE COUNTED

HEALTHY RAPID WEIGHT LOSS THE NATURAL WAY

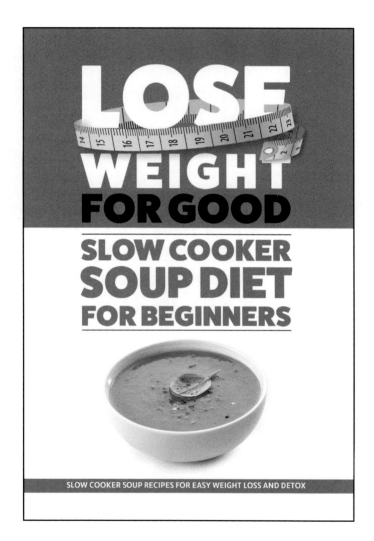